Thérèse *of* Lisieux
Living Justice

Dear Olivia.

I hope you find
St Therese interesting and
inspirational.

Blessed 1st Communion.

Ye-Ye + Grandma

SAINTS & VIRTUES

Thérèse *of* Lisieux
Living Justice

ave maria press AmP Notre Dame, Indiana

www.avemariapress.com

International Standard Book Number: 1-59471-059-7

Author of biography of St. Thérèse of Lisieux: Boniface Hanley, O.F.M.

Project Editor: Michael Amodei

Cover and text design by Brian C. Conley

Photos © Central Office de Lisieux

Printed and bound in the United States of America.

Contents

ST. THÉRÈSE *of* LISIEUX *9*

INTRODUCTION: *The* LITTLE FLOWER *11*

The LIFE *of* THÉRÈSE *15*

PRAY *With* THÉRÈSE *45*

Living JUSTICE *53*

Virtue

A virtue is a good habit that helps us to live the Christian life.

Justice

Justice is the virtue that guides the human will to give to God and others what is their due.

St. Thérèse of Lisieux

Thérèse Martin was born in
Alencon, France on January 2, 1873.

With her family, Thérèse moved to Lisieux in 1877.

Thérèse entered the Lisieux Carmel at age fifteen.

On September 30, 1897,
Thérèse died from the effects of tuberculosis.

Her short autobiography revealed her deep spirituality and her
simple life came to the attention of many.

Thérèse was canonized on May 17, 1925, by Pope Pius XI.

In 1997, Pope John Paul II declared St. Thérèse of Lisieux
a Doctor of the Church.

INTRODUCTION: *The* LITTLE *flower*

Jesus set before me the book of nature; I understood how all the flowers he has created are beautiful, how the splendor of the rose and the whiteness of the lily do not take away the perfume of the little violet or the simplicity of the daisy.

I understood that if all flowers wanted to be roses, nature would lose her springtime beauty, and the fields would no longer be decked out with little wild flowers.

And so it is in the world of souls, Jesus' garden.

He willed to create great souls comparable to lilies and roses, but he has created smaller ones and these must be content to be daisies or violets destined to give joy to God's glances when he looks down at his feet.

Perfection consists in doing God's will, in being what he wills us to be.

— ST. THÉRÈSE OF LISIEUX

*S*t. Thérèse of Lisieux is known as the "Little Flower," a symbol she devised for her life. She said she was like the little flower that survives the harshest conditions of winter only to appear again in the spring. And she understood that in God's plan for the world all people—like all flowers—have a place, even if their lives appear to be "little" in comparison to others. The task for us is to be as God intends for us to be.

Seeing yourself in God's plan is part of living the human virtue called *justice.*

The virtue of justice has two parts. The first involves giving God his due. God is the Creator and we are his creations. Being just means acknowledging our submissiveness to God, who is greater than we are. From this understanding of justice flows what is often called the "virtue of religion." To be just toward God we speak to him and listen to him in prayer. We receive his rules and we follow them. We understand that God has the right to make of us as he wishes.

The second part of justice relates to our treatment of other human beings. To be just, we must always consider the good of others. We put our own interests after theirs, respecting the common good above all. Ultimately, we are concerned not only with our own salvation but with the salvation of those we live beside.

Thérèse certainly was a model of justice in both of these ways, but she was especially so in the last third of her life. Born in 1873 in France, she lived only to the age of twenty-four. Her first years were lived as the highly favored youngest child of a widower whose four other surviving daughters spoiled her. Within this setting, she nurtured the grand idea that she would become a saint. By her early teen years she pursued the goal of joining her older sisters as a contemplative Carmelite nun.

It was in her last years at the convent that she devised her little way of living, which involved both giving back to God and loving the sisters in her community in what seemed the smallest of ways. When her prayers, reflections, and poetry were discovered in her handwritten biography after her death, Thérèse's little way became her road to sainthood and a model of living justly for all.

The following pages reveal a brief biographical sketch of St. Thérèse of Lisieux. First, *read about her life.* Try to take just one or two sittings over the course of one day to read pages 16-43.

Next, *pray with St. Thérèse.* Pages 46-51 offer a five day prayer meditation based on her life and writing.

Finally, *live the virtue of justice* as exemplified by St. Thérèse. Pages 56-61 share some ideas about how to do this. Keep a short journal to track how well you do.

The LIFE of THÉRÈSE

*L*ouis Martin loved to fish. Again and again he flicked his rod and cast his line above the sparkling waters of his favorite stream. With adept skill he tempted the wily and elusive trout to the bait. Louis' heart was at peace one summer afternoon in 1878 as he stood fishing in a stream near the village of Lisieux, France.

Louis was not alone that day. His little girl sat on the banks of the stream watching him. She was five and adored her father. She had been fishing, too, but grew tired of it. Now she sat, caught up in the quiet music of a summer afternoon: the running waters, the humming of insects, and the chirping of tiny birds. All these things delighted her. But the sight of her father fishing gave her the greatest joy.

The sun began to dip. Coolness spread across the flower-strewn meadow. Louis gathered up his rod and reel, and took his daughter by the hand. "Come, my little queen, we must go home."

The fisherman and his little daughter, Thérèse, walked hand in hand across the fields and up the hill toward their home in the village.

The Martins called their Lisieux home *Les Buissonnets* ("The Hedges"). It was a large and comfortable dwelling that easily satisfied the family's needs. Louis was a successful watchmaker by trade. He also skillfully managed his wife's lace business. But this was not exactly the life that Louis had planned long ago.

Louis Martin and Zelie Guerin

Born in 1823 into a family of soldiers, Louis spent his early years living at various French military posts. He absorbed a sense of order and discipline that military life

LOUIS MARTIN

ZELIE GUERIN

engenders. Yet, from an early age, Louis' temperament tended to things of the spirit.

At the age of twenty-two, Louis sought to enter the religious life. He approached the abbot at the monastery of the Augustinian Canons of the Great St. Bernard Hospice in the Alps. The blend of courage and charity of the monks appealed to Louis. He was also enamored with the monks' famous St. Bernard dogs that helped to rescue travelers trapped in the Alpine snow.

Alas, the Augustinian abbot insisted that Louis learn Latin in order to enter the monestary. Louis, whose bravery would have carried him to the heights of the Alps in search of a lost pilgrim, became lost himself in Latin syntax. His most determined efforts to learn the language failed. Dispirited and ill, he eventually abandoned his dreams of monastic life.

Eventually, Martin settled in the small French city of Alencon, where he began to learn the watch-making trade. He loved Alencon. It was a quiet place and Louis was a quiet man. A bountiful trout stream nearby offered Louis the opportunity to enjoy his favorite pastime. Alencon was also known throughout France as a center for lace-making. The lace makers were the most esteemed residents of Alencon. Their skill in producing the exquisite lace known as "Point d' Alencon" was greatly admired.

Zelie Guerin was one of Alencon's most talented lace makers. Like Louis, Zelie was raised in a military family. Looking back on her childhood, she called it "dismal." Her mother and father showed her little affection. Also like Louis, she desired the religious life but was turned away from the convent. That was when Zelie turned to lace-making. Richly talented, creative, eager, and endowed with common sense, Zelie started her own business that soon became a great success.

Louis Martin and Zelie Guerin eventually met in Alencon and on July 13, 1858, they married. Louis was thirty-four and Zelie was twenty-six. Their remarkable journey of family life had begun. Within the next fifteen years, Zelie bore nine children— seven girls and two boys. "We lived only for them. . . . They were all our happiness," Zelie wrote.

The Martin's delight in their children turned to shock and sorrow as tragedy mercilessly stalked their little ones. Within a three-year period, Zelie's two toddler boys, five-year-old daughter, and six-and-a-half-week-old infant girl all were lost to illness.

Zelie was left numbed with sadness. "I haven't a penny's worth of courage," she lamented. But her faith sustained her through these terrible ordeals. "When I closed the eyes of my dear little children and buried them, I felt sorrow through and through," Zelie wrote to her sister-in-law who had also lost an infant son. "People said to me 'It would have been better never to have had them.' I couldn't understand such language. My children were not lost forever; life is short and full of miseries and we shall find our little ones again up above."

The Martin's Youngest Child

Marie-Francoise-Thérèse Martin was born on January 2, 1873, the Martin's ninth and last child. She was fragile as an infant and the doctors feared for her life. The family, so used to death, was preparing for yet another blow. Zelie wrote of her three-month-old daughter: "I have no hope of saving her. The poor little thing suffers horribly. It breaks your heart to see her."

But the baby girl, called Thérèse , proved to be much tougher than anyone realized. She survived the illness. A year later, she was a "big baby, browned by the sun," according to her mother. Zelie also noted that "the baby is full of life, giggles a lot, and is a sheer joy to everyone."

Years later, Thérèse recalled her early years in Alencon in the same positive way. "All my life God surrounded me with love," she wrote. "My first memories are imprinted with the most tender smiles and caresses. Those were the sunny years of my childhood. My happy disposition contributed to making my life pleasant."

Death even seemed to bless the Martin household. Although suffering had left its mark on Louis and Zelie, it was not the scar of bitterness. The series of tragedies only intensified the love of husband and wife. They poured out their affection on their five surviving daughters: Marie, Pauline, Leonie, Celine, and baby Thérèse.

Thérèse's Personality Emerges

Thérèse was soon everyone's favorite, especially Zelie's. But even her mother was not blind to her baby's faults. Thérèse was, she wrote, "incredibly stubborn. When she has said 'no,' nothing will make her change her mind."

Thérèse's candor appeared early on and was unusual for a child. The little one would run to her mother and confess, "Mama, I hit Celine once—but I won't do it again."

Little Thérèse was blonde, blue-eyed, playful, affectionate, mischievous, stubborn, and alarmingly precocious. Her mother worried about her on the swing that Louis had built for the children. "When the swing doesn't go fast enough, she cries. We attached her to it with a rope, but, in spite of this, I'm still uneasy to see her perched so high."

Thérèse would throw huge temper tantrums. In a note that Zelie wrote to her daughter Pauline, she said: "Thérèse

ELEVEN-YEAR-OLD THÉRÈSE (RIGHT) AND HER FIFTEEN-YEAR-OLD SISTER CELINE, WHO WAS HER CONFIDANTE AND CONSTANT COMPANION.

flies into frightful tantrums; when things don't go just right and according to her way of thinking, she rolls on the floor in desperation like one without any hope. There are times when it gets to be too much for her and she literally chokes."

Yet Thérèse's bubbling laughter could make a gargoyle smile. Zelie added: "She is a nervous child, but she is very good, very intelligent, and remembers everything."

"I Choose All"

Because she felt no further use for it, Leonie, at age twelve, brought her doll dressmaking kit to six-year-old Celine and two-year-old Thérèse. Leonie had stuffed the basket full of materials for making new dresses.

"Choose what you wish, little sisters," invited Leonie. Celine took a little ball of wool that pleased her.

Thérèse simply said, "I choose all."

She accepted the basket and all its goods without ceremony. This incident reveals Thérèse's attitude toward life. She never did anything by halves; for her it was always all or nothing.

On Sundays, Papa and Mama Martin would take their daughters on walks. Thérèse loved the wide-open spaces and the beauty of the Alencon countryside. Frequently the walks tired little Thérèse and Papa Martin had to carry her home in his arms.

Thérèse's young life was idyllic. But the happy times were soon to end. The shadow of death once more crept over the Martin home.

Thérèse Grows Up

In August of 1877, when Thérèse was just four-years-old, Zelie Martin died. She had battled cancer for twelve years. The heart went out of the Martin home in Alencon.

It was shortly after his wife's death that Louis Martin moved his family to Lisieux and rented the house that he would name *Les Buissonnets*. Thérèse then entered what she called "the second and most painful" period of her life. "My happy disposition completely changed," she remembered. "I became timid and retiring, sensitive to an excessive degree."

Because she missed her mother so much, Louis and his daughters did all they could to help little Thérèse. They lavished affection and attention on her. At *Les Buissonnet*, under the tutelage of her sisters Marie and Pauline, Thérèse began her first schooling. Each day after her classes were over she joined her father in his study. Eventually the two would go for a walk. They would visit a different church each day and pray before the blessed sacrament. The bond between father and daughter grew stronger and stronger.

"How could I possible express the tenderness which Papa showered upon his queen?" Thérèse later recalled.

A Prodigy of the Spirit

Inside this precocious little child amazing things were happening. To appreciate Thérèse's interior growth, one fact must be understood: Thérèse was a child prodigy of the spirit much like Mozart was a child prodigy of music.

Whereas Mozart began his first European concert tour at age seven, at age three Thérèse began to refuse nothing, she said, "of what God asks me." Her intellectual and spiritual powers were developing at an amazing rate.

When Thérèse was five years old she vacationed with her family at the beaches of Trouville near their home. She later recalled what she was thinking as she viewed her first ocean sunset.

> *In the evening at that moment when the sun seems to bathe itself in the immensity of the waves, leaving a luminous trail behind, I went and sat on a huge rock with Pauline. I contemplated this luminous trail for a long time. It was to me the image of God's grace shedding its light across the path the white-sailed vessel (Thérèse herself) had to travel. . . . I made the resolution never to wander far from the path of Jesus, in order to travel peacefully toward the eternal shore.*

These reflections of Thérèse reveal the theme of exile that dominated her whole life. She said that the first word she learned to read was "heaven." From her childhood on, she interpreted her whole world as only the beginning, the glimpse of a glorious future. Sundays held tremendous significance for her. They were days of rest tinged with melancholy because they had to end. It was on Sunday evenings that Thérèse felt the pang of worldly exile: "I longed for the everlasting repose of heaven—that never-ending Sunday of the fatherland."

Still, at age five, Thérèse gave little outward indication of her intense inward life in the spirit. She was a pretty girl and vain enough to be pleased when people remarked on her beauty. Thérèse, on certain occasions, continued to have extreme temper tantrums. She recalled a scene that took place between herself and the nurse who cared for her, Victoire (the emphasis is her own):

I wanted an inkstand which was on the shelf of the fireplace in the kitchen. Being too little to take it down, I very nicely asked Victoire to give it to me. But she refused, telling me to get up on a chair. I took a chair without saying a word, but thinking she wasn't too nice; wanting to make her feel it, I searched out in my little head what offended me the most. She often called me a "little brat" when she was annoyed at me and humbled me very much. So before jumping off my chair, I turned around with dignity and said, "Victoire, you are a brat!" Then I made my escape leaving Victoire to meditate on the profound statement I had just made.... I thought, if Victoire didn't want to stretch her big arm to do me a little service, she merited the title "brat."

More Sad Days

In October of 1881 Louis enrolled his youngest daughter as a day boarder at Lisieux's Benedictine Abbey. Thérèse hated the place and described her five years there as the "saddest" of her life. Classes bored her. Because of her intelligence, the nuns advanced the eight-year-old to classes with fourteen-year-olds. But still she was bored. Her keenness aroused the envy of many fellow pupils, and Thérèse paid dearly for her academic success. The ordinary games and dances of other children held little interest for her. She was uncomfortable with most children and seemed to be at ease only with her own sisters and very few others.

Of all her sisters, Thérèse was closest to Pauline, her first teacher and hero. Thérèse also thought of Pauline as her second mother. When Thérèse was nine, Pauline told her that she was leaving home to enter the Carmelite convent in Lisieux. Thérèse was stunned. She later described her sorrow:

I was about to lose my second mother. Ah, how can I express the anguish of my heart! In one instant I understood what life was; until then I had never seen it so sad, but it appeared to me in all its reality and I saw that it was nothing but continual suffering and separation. I shed bitter tears.

It was also shortly after Pauline's departure that Thérèse determined to join her at Lisieux's Carmelite convent. She approached the prioress and sought entrance into the community. Carefully little Thérèse explained she wished to enter, not for Pauline's sake, but for Jesus' sake. The prioress advised her to return when she grew up.

During the winter following Pauline's entrance into the Carmelite convent, Thérèse fell seriously ill. Doctors diagnosed her sickness as everything from a nervous breakdown to a kidney infection. She blamed it on the devil. Whatever it was, the doctors of her time were unable to either diagnose or treat it. She suffered intensely from constant headaches and insomnia during this time. She also had fits of fever and trembling and suffered from cruel hallucinations. Thérèse later wrote about one of these bouts of delirium:

I was absolutely terrified by everything: My bed seemed to be surrounded by frightful precipices; some nails in the wall of the room took on the appearance of big, black, charred fingers, making me cry out in fear. One day, while Papa was looking at me and smiling, the hat in his hand was suddenly transformed into some indescribable dreadful shape and I showed such great fear that poor Papa left the room sobbing.

Then, just as suddenly, in May of 1883 the illness came to an end. Thérèse claimed she was healed miraculously when a statue of the Blessed Mother smiled at her. During her long illness, Thérèse's resolve to join the Carmelites grew even stronger: "I am convinced that the thought of one day becoming a Carmelite made me live."

Glory Through Suffering

After her illness, Thérèse was more determined than ever to do something great for God and for humanity. She thought of herself as a new Joan of Arc, dedicated not only to the rescue of France, but of the whole world. Boldly, she concluded, "I was born for glory." And thus another theme of Thérèse's life manifested itself. She perceived her life's mission as one of helping all people toward salvation. She was to accomplish this by becoming a saint. Thérèse understood that her glory would be hidden from the world until God wished to reveal it.

Even at the age of ten, Thérèse was intelligent enough to realize that she could not become a saint without suffering. What she did not realize was just how much suffering she would have to endure to win her glory.

Shortly after her First Communion and Confirmation in the spring of 1884, Thérèse experienced a peculiarly vicious attack of scruples. She lived in constant fear of committing a sin; the most abhorrent and absurd thoughts disturbed her peace. She wept often. Headaches plagued her once again. Louis finally removed her from the abbey school and provided private tutoring for her. This new round of mental torture continued for a year and a half.

After midnight Mass on Christmas in 1886, Thérèse's shadow of self-doubt, depression, and uncertainty suddenly lifted, leaving her in possession of a new calm and inner conviction. The third and last period of her life was about to begin. She called it her life's "most beautiful" period.

Thérèse was consumed, like Jesus, with a thirst for souls. Convinced that her prayers and sufferings could bring people to Christ, she asked Jesus to give her some sign that she was right. He did.

THÉRÈSE HOLDS REPRESENTATION OF CHRIST AS A CHILD AND THE CHRIST OF THE HOLY FACE. A MONTH AFTER THE PICTURE WAS TAKEN, SHE WAS TAKEN ILL AND ENTERED THE CONVENT INFIRMARY.

In the early summer of 1887 a criminal, Henri Pranzini, was convicted of the murder of two women and a child. He was sentenced to the guillotine. The convicted man, according to newspaper reports, showed no inclination to repent. Thérèse began to pray nonstop for Pranzini's conversion. She prayed for weeks and had Mass offered for him. But there was no change in the attitude of the condemned man. The French newspaper *La Croix* noted how Pranzini had at first refused to go to confession. However, as the executioner was about to put his head onto the guillotine block, the criminal seized the crucifix that a priest offered him and, the newspaper noted, "kissed the sacred wounds three times."

Thérèse read the news with great joy and thanksgiving. She interpreted Pranzini's final act as a sign that Jesus was pleased with her plan to give her life in prayer for sinners.

Thérèse Makes a Request

Marie, the oldest Martin daughter, joined Pauline at the Lisieux Carmelite convent in 1886. Leonie Martin entered the Visitation Convent at Caen the following year. Thérèse then sought permission from her father to join Marie and Pauline at the Lisieux convent. Louis was probably expecting the request, but it saddened him nevertheless. Three of his girls had already left home and entered religious life. But, characteristically generous, he not only granted Thérèse's request but worked zealously so that she could realize it.

Thérèse was not yet fifteen when she approached the Carmelite authorities again seeking permission to enter the convent. Again she was refused. The priest-director advised her to return when she was twenty-one. "Of course," he added, "you can always see the bishop. I am only his delegate." The priest did not realize what kind of girl he was dealing with!

Thérèse went with her father to see the bishop shortly afterwards. To his dying day Bishop Hugonin of Bayeux never forgot Thérèse. She had put up her hair, thinking this would make her look older. (The bishop laughed and recounted this with Thérèse in later years.) She put her surprising request before him. "You are not yet fifteen and you wish this?" the bishop questioned.

"I have wished it since the day of reason," young Thérèse declared. Louis' support of her request amazed the bishop. He had never seen anything like it. "A father as eager to give his child to God," he remarked, "as this child was eager to offer herself to God."

Although charmed by her, Bishop Hugonin did not immediately grant Thérèse's request. He wanted time to consider it and advised Thérèse and Louis that he would write them regarding his decision.

Thérèse decided that if her request to the bishop failed, she would go to the pope himself. Thus in November of 1887 Louis took Thérèse and Celine to Rome with a group of French pilgrims. Catholics from all over the world were journeying to Rome to celebrate Pope Leo XIII's fiftieth anniversary of ordination. The trip was memorable for Thérèse in many ways. In Rome she was enamored with the Colosseum. Its history as a site of Christian martyrdom stirred the roots of her very being. She and Celine, ignoring regulations prohibiting visitors from descending through the ruined structure to the arena floor, sneaked away from the tour group, climbed across the barriers, and went down the runs to kneel and pray on the Colosseum floor. Gathering up a few stones as relics, they slipped back to the tour. No one, except their father, noted their absence.

The great day moment with Pope Leo XIII came at the end of their week in Rome. Thérèse later described what happened:

They told us on the pope's behalf that it was forbidden to speak as this would prolong the audience too much. I turned toward my dear Celine for advice: "Speak!" she said. A moment later I was at the Holy Father's feet. . . . Lifting tear-filled eyes to his face I cried out: "Most Holy Father, I have a great favor to ask you! Holy Father, in honor of your jubilee, permit me to enter Carmel at the age of fifteen."

Father Revrony, the leader of the French pilgrimage, stared at this bold little girl, in surprise and displeasure.

"Most Holy Father," the priest said coldly, "this is a child who wants to enter Carmel at the age of fifteen. The superiors are considering the matter at the moment."

"Well, my child," Pope Leo replied, "do what the superiors tell you."

Thérèse rested her hands on the Pope's knees and continued:

I made a final effort saying, "Oh, Holy Father, if you say 'yes,' everybody will agree." He gazed at me steadily speaking these words and stressing each syllable: "Go—go—you will enter if God wills it."

Thérèse did not want to leave the Holy Father's presence and the guards had to lift her up and carry her to the door.

Thérèse Enters Carmel

On New Year's Day, 1888, a day before her fifteenth birthday, the prioress of the Lisieux Carmel told Thérèse she would be received into the convent in April.

The only cloud on Thérèse's horizon was the worsening condition of her father, who was growing senile. He once wandered from his home and was lost for three days. Celine remained at *Les Buissonnets* to care for Louis during this long and final illness.

In August, after a series of strokes, Louis became paralyzed. Years before, when Thérèse was just a toddler, she had a vision of a stooped and twisted man in the family garden. She had called out, "Papa, Papa," even though Louis had been away in Alencon on business. Now the meaning of her vision became apparent. Louis' health rallied briefly and he was able to attend the ceremonies of Thérèse's clothing in the Carmelite habit in January of 1889. Later that same year Louis had a mental breakdown and had to be hospitalized. He was able to visit Carmel one more time in 1892. Louis died peacefully in 1894. After his death, Celine, too, joined her three sisters at Carmel, the fifth daughter to become a nun.

THÉRÈSE PORTRAYS JOAN OF ARC IN A RELIGIOUS PLAY PERFORMED FOR THE NUNS IN HER CONVENT.

Thérèse spent the last nine years of her life at the Lisieux Carmel. Her fellow sisters recognized her as a good nun, but nothing more. She was conscientious and capable. Sister Thérèse worked in the sacristy, cleaned the dining room, painted pictures, composed pious playlets for the sisters, wrote poems, and loved the intense community prayer life of the cloister. Her superiors appointed her to instruct the novices of the community. Exteriorly, there was nothing remarkable about this Carmelite nun.

The Story of a Soul

In her interior life, Thérèse Martin was caught up in an exchange of love with Christ so dynamic and profound that her whole being was transformed. Like St. Paul, she could say, "I live, not now I, but Christ lives in me." The world would never have known about this hidden interior life except for the fact that Thérèse's sister, Pauline, who had become prioress of the Lisieux Carmel, ordered her to write an autobiography.

Thérèse's autobiography, called *The Story of a Soul*, was published in 1898, one year after her death. The two thousand copies that comprised the first printing has swelled to multiple printings and millions of copies. The book has been translated into over forty languages. Thérèse's life story has captivated men and women of every state and condition of life. To this day it continues to touch the hearts of all who read it.

The Story of a Soul reveals Thérèse Martin as a young women who was sensitive, charmingly candid, endowed with a sense of humor, and keenly responsive to people and nature. In many ways, Thérèse was a very unconventional nun. She did not care for long spiritual discourses; she abhorred retreats. She loved the Blessed Mother but could not stand saying the rosary.

In an age when frequent reception of Holy Communion was discouraged, she remarked that Christ did not come to the Eucharist to remain in a golden ciborium.

Seeking the Depths of Love and Life

Love is what Thérèse Martin was all about. From her earliest days she was fascinated by love and determined to plumb its depths regardless of personal cost. She was driven by a ferocious desire to unlock nothing else but the mystery of life itself. "How can a soul as imperfect as mine aspire to the possession of love?" she wondered. It was through her determination that she was able to reach out and love.

The well-known symbol Thérèse chose for her life was the "little flower." The symbol is deceptive. Her purpose in using it was to explain that, like the tiny wild flower growing in the forest, she survived and indeed flourished through all the seasons of the year—through the warmth of spring and summer as well as the wind and snow of fall and winter. It was her way of saying: "I am a lot stronger than I look. Don't let appearances fool you."

Who was the source of her strength? She claimed that it was no one else but Jesus. She interpreted her whole life and all its events as Jesus teaching and revealing himself to her. Jesus watched over her, supported her when her mother died, forgave her sins, and instructed her. During the times when she needed him most, Jesus was silent; he slept in the boat during the frequent storms of her life. But without words, Jesus taught her the sure path to follow—abandonment to God's will. He did not require great deeds, but only her love. Each day was a gift from God. Thérèse expresses this idea in a poem that she wrote:

My life is a moment,
a passing hour.
My life is a moment,
which flits away from me.
O my God, you know that
for loving you on earth,
I have only today.
What does it matter, Lord,
if the future is bleak!
I cannot pray for tomorrow's needs . . .
keep my heart pure,
keep me in your shade just for today.

Thérèse developed her doctrine of abandonment and love at a time when Christianity instead stressed the fear of God. She bravely flew in the face of religious convention because she could not accept that God would ever reject his children.

Thérèse was moved by the Suffering Servant passages from the book of Isaiah. Isaiah said that the servant would be crushed with suffering, but that through this one innocent man's wounds all people would be healed. The gospels developed Isaiah's teaching further, by describing Christ as the Suffering Servant. It is through Christ and his suffering that God brings healing to us all.

One passage, from Isaiah 53, Thérèse particularly took to heart:

He was spurned and avoided by men,
a man of suffering accustomed to infirmity,
One of those from whom men hide their faces,
spurned, and we held him in no esteem (Isaiah 53:3).

Thérèse wrote, "I desire that, like the face of Jesus, my face be truly hidden, that no one on earth would know me. I thirsted after suffering and longed to be forgotten." In the Carmelite community Thérèse took as her name "Sister Thérèse of the Child Jesus and the Holy Face."

Abandonment to Christ

Thérèse felt that Jesus was calling her to participate in the continuation of his redemptive suffering and death. Like Jesus, she recognized that souls were to be won through the mystery of suffering and it was to this that she dedicated her life. She wanted to love people the way Christ loved them, but she knew that this was impossible. And yet this was the command Jesus had given. So, the only way for her to fulfill the commandment would be to let Jesus take possession of her and then to have him love others through her.

Thus Thérèse had to abandon herself to Christ. She came before him with all of her faults and failings. She was not ashamed of her failings, knowing that Jesus was merciful and would quickly forgive them.

Thérèse remained aware of her smallness:

> *It is impossible for me to grow up, so I must bear with myself such as I am with all my imperfections. But I want to see out a means of going to heaven by a little way, a way that is very straight, very short, and totally new.*

Thérèse went on to describe how she imagined herself reaching Jesus by riding an elevator to him (much easier than climbing stairs):

> *I wanted to find an elevator which would raise me to Jesus, for I am too small to climb the rough stairway of perfection. I searched then in the Scriptures for some sign of this elevator, the object of my desires and I read these words coming from the mouth of Eternal Wisdom: "Whoever is a little one let him come to me." The elevator which must raise me to heaven is your arms, O Jesus, and for this I have no need to grow up, but rather I have to remain little and become this more and more.*

And so Thérèse abandoned herself to Jesus and her life became a continual acceptance of the will of the Lord.

The Lord, it seems, did not demand great things of her. But she felt incapable of the tiniest charity, of the smallest expression of concern, patience, or understanding. So she surrendered her life to Christ with the hope that he would act through her. She again mirrored perfectly the words of St. Paul who wrote "I can do all things in him who strengthens me." "All things" consisted of almost everything she was called upon to do in the daily grind of life.

All Things

Thérèse leaned over a wash pool with a group of sisters, laundering handkerchiefs. One of the sisters splashed the hot, dirty wash water at Thérèse's face, not once, not twice, but continually. The terrible-tempered Thérèse was near to throwing one of her best tantrums. But she said nothing. Christ helped her to accept this lack of consideration on the part of her fellow sister. And by doing so she found peace.

Another time, she was moved by her youthful idealism to help Sister St. Pierre, a crotchety, older nun who refused to let old age keep her from convent activities. "You move too fast," the old nun complained as Thérèse walked by her side. Thérèse slowed down. "Well, come on," Sister St. Pierre then urged. "I don't feel your hand. You have let go of me and I am going to fall. I was right when I said you were too young to help me." Thérèse took it all and managed to smile. This was her little way.

Another nun made strange, clacking noises in the chapel. Perhaps she was either toying with her rosary or was afflicted by ill-fitting dentures. Thérèse could not say. The clacking really bothered Thérèse, grinding into her brain. Impatient Thérèse

IN THE COMMUNITY LAUNDERETTE, THÉRÈSE, SECOND FROM THE LEFT IN THE FRONT ROW, CARRIES A WOODEN PADDLE TO POUND THE LINENS.

was sweating in frustration. She tried to shut out the nun's noise, but unsuccessfully. So instead she made a concert out of the clacking and offered it as a prayer to Jesus. "I assure you," Thérèse dryly remarked, "that was no prayer of quiet!"

Thérèse, the great mystic saint, fell asleep frequently at prayer. She was embarrassed by her inability to remain awake during her hours in chapel with the religious community. Finally, in perhaps her most charming and accurate characterization of the little way, she noted that just as parents love their children as much asleep as awake so too God loved her even though she often slept during prayer time.

Thérèse spoke bravely about wanting to join Christ's redemptive suffering. In June of 1895, she offered herself to merciful love in an act of complete sacrifice. At the urging of her superiors, Thérèse united her prayer life and sacrifices and dedicated them to certain missionaries out in the world. In the solitude of her cell at the Lisieux convent, she joined her prayers and her life with the prayers and work of the missionaries.

God responded by filling her with a happiness, joy, and delight in his presence that she had never known before. Thérèse was giving up her life for souls.

Thérèse's Way of the Cross

Thérèse was living in complete union with Christ as she remained mostly in solitude. But as the last year and a half of her life began, she started to walk a dreadful Way of the Cross. Sometime during the evening and morning hours of Holy Thursday and Good Friday in 1896, the tuberculosis which had been a minor affliction to her in the previous two years caused hemorrhaging.

For Thérèse, the bloodletting was a sign that Christ would soon take her to himself and that her days of exile on earth would soon be over. She said: "I was interiorly persuaded that Jesus, on the anniversary of the day of his own death, wanted to make me his first call. It was like a sweet and distant murmur which was announcing the arrival of the Bridegroom."

For the next year and a half, the tuberculosis tortured Thérèse's body. But this suffering paled in comparison to the mental torture which she had to endure. She began to go into a frightful trial of faith. She described it as a torment, a darkness that blotted out the presence of God in her life. She could find no image of God, her hope of heaven disappeared, her faith weakened, and she seemed to be on the verge of breaking. She wrote:

The darkness, borrowing the voice of sinners, says to me in mocking tones: "You are dreaming of the light, a country perfumed by the sweetest scents; you are dreaming of the eternal possession of the Creator of all these marvels; you believe you will go out one day from the fog that surrounds you. Advance, advance, rejoice in death which will give you, not what you have hoped for, but a night still more profound, the night of nothingness.

Thérèse struggled with the largest questions of life, including its very meaning. She was stripped of everything— her health, her happiness. She was completely dependent upon others as she was forced by her illness to live the life of an invalid. She was only twenty-three years old. She was mocked by the possibility that all the things she had believed in might be false, that her little way, like everything else in her life, just led to a dead end. She was crushed between the desire to find God and the despair of not doing so. She seemed incapable of living one more day.

As the second part of her biography describes, with her brilliance, courage, and characteristic verve, Thérèse swept aside death and chose once more her little way of abandonment to Christ. She was reassured in what she had come to learn through her life, that she was, indeed, the little one whom God, in his mercy, embraced.

Thérèse also discovered in her illness that "to love" means to admit the need for love and to express that need in prayer to Christ, who *is* Love embodied. In doing this she found that love could sustain her. Indeed, as her suffering led her closer to death, she said to her sister Pauline, "I no longer have any great desire except that of loving to the point of dying of love."

Thérèse taught that God puts within each person the desire for God and that only he can satisfy this desire. To accept any other source for human happiness only leads to despair.

Sickness Leads to Death and New Life

In July of 1897, Thérèse was brought to the convent infirmary. She was hemorrhaging continually. At the end of the month she received the sacrament of anointing and in the middle of August, she received Communion for the final time. Her last agony was frightening.

Thérèse had a premonition that her death would not end her influence on earth. "How unhappy I shall be in heaven," she said, "If I cannot do little favors on earth for those whom I love."

She indicated that, with her death, her mission would begin, that is, "my mission of making God loved as I love him, to give

During her last months Thérèse often rested in the Carmelite cloister. "I go to him with confidence and love," were the last words she wrote.

my little way to souls. If God answers my request, my heaven will be spent on earth up until the end of the world. Yes, I want to spend my heaven in doing good upon earth."

Her illness reached a horrible climax between August 22 and 27. The tuberculosis had attacked not only her lungs but had infected her whole body. Thérèse suffered violently with each breath she took. She cried out from the pain. "What a grace to have the faith," she remarked. "If I did not have any faith, I would have inflicted death on myself without a moment's hesitation."

Somehow she survived this terrible time and lasted several more weeks. She retained her sense of humor throughout. And yet, at the same time, she remained deeply troubled by an interior trial. She complained, "Must one love God and the Blessed Virgin so much, and still have thoughts like this?

She thought of a black hole in the garden and told Pauline, "I'm in a hole just like that, soul and body. Ah, yes, what darkness. However, I am at peace."

The end came on September 30, 1897. Pauline related her last minutes:

> *I was all alone with her when, at about 4:30 p.m., I guessed by her sudden pallor that her end was approaching. Mother Prioress returned, and very soon the community was reassembled around her bed. She smiled at the sisters but did not speak until the moment of death . . . it was becoming increasingly difficult for her to breathe, and she uttered involuntary cries while trying to catch her breath.*

Next, Thérèse implored the prioress: "Mother! Isn't it the agony? Am I not going to die?"

"Yes, my poor child, it is the agony," Mother Prioress replied, "but God wills perhaps to prolong it for several hours."

Thérèse was holding the crucifix in her hand. Gazing at it, she said, "Oh! I love him." And a moment later, "My God, I love you."

Bystanders maintained that Thérèse's face again took on the appearance it had when she was in full health. She closed her eyes and expired. It was 7:20 p.m. She had written a few months before her death to a missionary who expressed anxiety about her illness: "I am not dying. I am entering into life."

Within a few years, pilgrims began making their way to the grave of Thérèse to pray.

In 1923, Pope Pius XI beatified Thérèse. On May 17, 1925, he canonized her in Rome.

In 1997, Pope John Paul II named Thérèse a Doctor of the Church.

Her autobiography, *The Story of a Soul*, remains a bestseller.

Pray With
THÉRÈSE

Prayers and Thoughts for the Day
(adapted from the poems and letters of St. Thérèse)

- Allow ten minutes for quiet prayer at the beginning of each of the five days.

- Pray the Morning Prayer.

- Read and reflect on the Thought for the Day and its meaning for your life.

- Commit the Thought for the Day to memory.

- At the end of the day, reserve fifteen minutes for journaling and prayer. In your journal, reflect on and write about times when you were able to serve God and others through Thérèse's little way.

- Conclude with the Evening Prayer.

*day*ONE

Morning Prayer

Jesus, I love you,
come and be with me today.
I offer all of my day's tasks to you.
Help me to recognize your presence in the people I meet
   today,
be they the stranger in the street,
a teacher that I struggle with,
my friends who bring joy to my day,
or in my family whom deep down I love.
Come and live in my heart!
Smile tenderly on me,
today, dear Lord, today.

Evening Prayer

O sweet Virgin Mother,
you shine with the light of Christ
and guide me on my way to him.
Let me rest, dear Mother, under the veil of your protection
and wake to serve your Son again.

THOUGHT FOR THE DAY
*Our Lord does not look so much at the greatness of our
actions, nor even at their difficulty, but at the love
with which we do them.*

---

*day*TWO

Morning Prayer

Incarnate Word, live in my soul.
Spirit of Love, enkindle my will to return your love
and draw me to my Father.
Stay with me today, Blessed Trinity.
Let me live by your love.

Evening Prayer

Dear Lord, to live in your love is to know no fear.
The fire of your love has taken away dark memories
and purified me of my sins.
The fire of your love carries me through the day
and protects me at night.
Be with me always.

THOUGHT FOR THE DAY
Do all that you do with love.

---

*day*THREE

Morning Prayer

Heavenly Father, in spite of my smallness,
I still dare to gaze upon the vastness of your love.
Envelop me.
Nourish me with your divine care.
Bring me to greatness in your loving eyes.

Evening Prayer

O beloved Lord, weak, so weak, am I.
Though my heart feels like a mighty treasure,
it is contained in a fragile vase.
Not yet have I been perfected in your grace.
Come to me, Lord, when I fail.
Protect me and give me strength.
Bring me home to your love.

THOUGHT FOR THE DAY
Nothing is small in the eyes of God.

---

*day*FOUR

Morning Prayer

Christ Jesus, help me to simplify my life.
The clutter of false goals and unimportant tasks
interferes with me knowing and loving you.
Keep me on the road leading to you,
and take away my extra burdens.
Lighten my load of this world so that I might
take on the challenges of being your follower.

Evening Prayer

Lord, give me the courage to remain near you
though stormy waves crash against my soul.
Call me to you and I will come.
Bring me the gift of faith
and I will reach out to you in love.

THOUGHT FOR THE DAY
*You cannot be half a saint. You must be a whole saint
or nothing at all.*

---

*day*FIVE

Morning Prayer

Dear Jesus, only you I seek,
There is no reward but you.
I reject the false promises of the world:
the pleasure of the quick fix,
the security based on brute force,
or the pride-filled thoughts where
I am everyone's favorite or
am recognized as superior to all those around me.
Help me reject all these easy illusions.
Rather, bring on the pain of being your disciple,
bring on the sacrifice of all true love.
Then, only then, will I gain you, dear Lord.

Evening Prayer

O Jesus, I calmly wait to be with you in heaven,
for all pain to be lifted
and to be sheltered in your care.
When that day comes, hope will be no more,
for all hope will have found fulfillment.
Bring me to your heavenly mansion
where I will die no more but only
live in you.

> ### THOUGHT FOR THE DAY
> *Fear only one thing: choosing your own will. Let Christ
> take your will and then choose as he chooses.*

Living
Justice

*J*ustice consists in giving God and others their due. Justice given to God is the "virtue of religion." It is our humble response to his laws and providence in our lives. We talk to God in prayer and listen to his response.

Being just always means respecting the rights of others. Being just means being fair.

As you have grown up, you have likely witnessed plenty of examples of unfairness.

For example, a kid may have cheated in class and received a better grade than you and others who didn't cheat.

Or, you may have been cut from a team while a less talented relative of the coach made it.

On a larger scale, there is a great amount of injustice in the world. There is an overwhelming imbalance in the world's wealth. The top twenty percent on the world's economic ladder possess sixty times the wealth and goods of the bottom twenty percent. Nearly 1.2 billion people live in absolute poverty.

The virtue of justice calls on us to correct these imbalances, both the small and the large.

St. Thérèse lived out her little way of justice in the Carmel convent of Lisieux. This way of living was not about doing extraordinary things, but rather about doing the simple everyday chores and interactions with others with love. She found God's face in all people and in all situations.

Thérèse also modeled the virtue of justice necessary to correct these larger world problems. It is interesting that in spite of spending nearly all of her life in Lisieux and her last years in a convent, Thérèse is the Church's patron saint of foreign missions.

Why? For one, Thérèse always dreamed of being a missionary. By the time she came to accept her vocation at Carmel, Thérèse continued to participate in the missionary work of the church through her own prayer and sacrifice at the convent. From the model of her life, discovered in *The Story of a Soul*, she brought the life of Christ to countless others. She showed that all Christians, not just those who travel overseas, are called to do the work of missionaries, to work for justice for all while offering back to God what is his due.

You are called to live the virtue of justice, like St. Thérèse.

Spend some time reading and reflecting on the following twenty-five project ideas. Some of these involve ways to live the virtue of justice in your own smaller sphere. Others may seem larger in scale. Choose two or three of the projects to enact.

Remember Thérèse's little way. Whichever projects you choose, big or small, will have meaning and purpose for God and for others when done in the spirit of justice and love.

Twenty-Five Justice Project Ideas for Teens

The following ideas are intended to whet your appetite for justice. Before doing any justice project, research the issue you plan to work on. There are many websites devoted to justice projects, service learning, and community service.

After your research, determine whether you will take the lead role in developing the project, work with an existing agency, or serve with a group of your peers.

Also, remember: Justice begins at home. Employ the little way of St. Thérèse in all that you do.

1. Rent and view the movie *Pay It Forward*. In the movie, a boy decides that if he does three good things for others and tells them to "pass it on," the amount of good and good deeds will multiply unbelievably. Choose how you can live the message of the film. See the Pay It Forward Foundation at www.payitforwardfoundation.org for more information.

2. Join a peace organization. *Pax Christi* has been a prominent Catholic peace and justice movement since 1945. Visit their website at www.paxchristiusa.org for ideas about how to join and what you can do for peace after you join.

3. Volunteer at a local hospital. Most hospitals allow teens fourteen years and older to help deliver flowers, books, and mail to patients. You may also be able to assist with office tasks and other deliveries.

4. Be a translator for local agencies that serve the poor. For example, you might be able to translate a flyer advertising meals and services for the homeless from English to Spanish.

5. Coordinate a "Senior Home Repair Project" for older adults in your parish. Set a menu of repairs you and/or your group are willing and able to complete (e.g., painting, yard maintenance, gutter clearing, etc.). Advertise the services to seniors in your parish. Schedule work teams. Arrange for supplies. Begin!

6. Go out to lunch with a peer or younger student who is in need of a friend.

7. Interview at least three adults from your school, neighborhood, or parish about possible service project ideas. Choose at least one project to enact.

8. Youth Service America is an alliance of over three hundred agencies designed to provide volunteer opportunities for people from ages five to twenty-five. Visit the Youth Service America website at www.ysa.org. Within the site, type in your zip code to find out about service opportunities in your area.

9. Collect used and new athletic equipment for those in need. Donate the equipment locally (e.g., to the Boys and Girls Club) or globally (the USA Freedom Corps recently collected thousands of soccer balls for the people in Iraq).

10. With the help of your local St. Vincent de Paul Agency, research statistics about the poor and immigrants in your area. Also, speak with a representative to find out how you can volunteer.

11. Form a welcoming committee for teenagers new to your parish or school. Oftentimes a parish will go out of their way to welcome new families. Make the task of your committee to specifically address welcoming *teenagers*. This could mean inviting the new teen to a party you arrange or to attend a game or movie with a group of teens from the parish or school.

12. Knit sweaters for needy children around the world. The Guideposts Sweater Project helps to provide an overview of the project, a pattern and knitting instructions, and where to donate the finished sweaters. See www.guideposts.com for more information.

13. Donate blood to a local blood bank or to the American Red Cross.

14. Say "hello" to at least five people you usually never speak to.

15. Offer your services at a local homeless shelter. Baby-sit, read to younger children, or help with homework. Visit the Housing and Urban Development website (www.hud.gov/index.html) for more information about homelessness and for ways you can help.

16. With your family, take the Family Pledge of Non-Violence, adapted by the Institute for Peace and Justice. It can be downloaded at www.ipj-ppj.org.

17. Offer a novena (nine consecutive days of prayer) to St. Thérèse. Pray for the following intentions: faith, hope, love, submission, patience, simplicity, humility, serving others, and a happy death. Many websites devoted to St. Thérèse include sample novenas.

18. Support the right to life of the unborn. Participate in a Right to Life march. Alternatively, directly provide support to pregnant teens. For example, gather and transport school homework assignments to pregnant teens or provide volunteer assistance at shelters for women.

19. Attend a work camp, usually held during the summer months. Teens do work for families in needy areas of the United States. Visit the Catholic Heart Workcamp website at www.heartworkcamp.com for more information on how you and others from your parish or school can participate.

20. Provide five hours of free baby-sitting to a family you might usually charge.

21. Pray for peace. Make a conscious effort over the course of one week to avoid swearing, cursing, and any other harsh words that can be construed as a violent or aggressive response.

22. Work with physically or emotionally disabled children. Check to see if there is a Special Olympics qualifying meet in your area. Or, volunteer to help with the Challenger Program of Little League baseball.

23. Write a letter (not an e-mail) to a relative or friend telling them about your life, inquiring about their life, and telling how much you care about them.

24. Research information about Heifer International (see www.heifer.org). This is an organization that purchases livestock that can be raised as a food source for people around the world. One possible project is to initiate a penny collection among classmates, parishioners, and neighbors. Collect unwanted pennies. Donate the profits you raise to Heifer International.

25. Sit before the Blessed Sacrament. Pray for justice for all.

If you found *Thérèse of Lisieux* interesting, learn more with *Simply Surrender*

Simply Surrender

Based on the Little Way of Thérèse of Lisieux

Learn about Thérèse of Lisieux through her autobiography *The Little Way*. Thérèse's *Little Way* reveals a path of childlike surrender to God that has been embraced by millions around the world. Ponder the depths of Thérèse's simple insights and discover the power they hold for you, too.

This is one of the 17 books from the popular series *30 Days With a Great Spiritual Teacher* authored by John Kirvan which can be seen at www.avemariapress.com.
ISBN: 0-87793-590-4 / 216 pages / $8.95

Learn more about the virtues with the next book in the Saints and Virtues series—*Francis of Assisi*

SAINTS VIRTUES *The Saints and Virtues Series...*booklets featuring illustrated biographies of popular heroic Christians, prayers, and service activities that combine to create a resource that brings alive the Catholic faith for teens and shows that the virtues can be lived by everyday people.

Francis of Assisi

Living Fortitude

Fortitude enables us to conquer our fears, even the fear of death, in the name of our beliefs.

Francis' love of God and his faith in the spiritual life gave him the strength, or fortitude, to follow God even when his parents abandoned him. Francis remains a spiritual and human example of the importance in standing firm in your beliefs—even in situations that may seem unpleasant or possibly deadly. The prayers and service activities demonstrate to students that they have the strength to stand behind their beliefs and shows how they can integrate the virtue of fortitude into their own lives.
ISBN: 1-59471-060-0 / 64 pages / 6" x 9" / $5.50

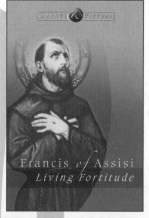

KEYCODE: F0A01050000